D1475583

Sonnets

With Sasha

A Collection of Best-loved, Heartfelt and Inspirational
Poetry with an Album of Celebrated Sasha Dolls,
Created by Swiss Artist Sasha Morgenthaler,
Interpreted by Their Most Passionate Collectors.

MCNAE, MARLIN & MACKENƷIE, LTD.
BOOK AND PERIODICAL PUBLISHERS
GLASGOW • NEW YORK • LOS ANGELES
QUEENS ROAD, GLASGOW, LANARKSHIRE G42 8OO SCOTLAND

ISBN-13: 978-1-68454-098-3
ISBN-10: 1-68454-098-4

Front Cover – Repainted Sasha Doll and photograph by Shelly Baxter. Back Cover – Repainted and rewigged Dolls "Edith", "Clarisse", and "Gertie" by Janet Myhill Dabbs were inspired by an original Studio Doll made by Sasha Morgenthaler. Photograph by Kendal Hackney.

For more information on Sasha Morgenthaler and Sasha Dolls, please visit
http://sashamorgenthaler.org
www.sashadolluk.co.uk
www.sashadoll.com
www.thesashaemporium.org
www.sashadoll.net
www.kendalssashabrood.wordpress.com
And the following groups on Facebook
Sasha Doll Study Group
Sasha Doll UK
Sasha Dolls Bazaar Dolls
Sasha Dolls Bazaar Outfits
Scenes of Sasha
Sasha Morgenthaler Dolls

Dedicated to Susanna E. Lewis
Textile and knitwear artist, author, researcher,
Sasha Doll collector and enthusiast, and friend to many.

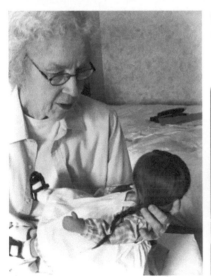

Bottom Photographs by Cathy Himmel

Sasha Morgenthaler   © *Godi Leiser*

Do not go gentle into that good night
by Dylan Thomas

Do not go gentle into that good night,
Old age should burn and rave at close of day;
Rage, rage against the dying of the light.

Though wise men at their end know dark is right,
Because their words had forked no lightning they
Do not go gentle into that good night.

Good men, the last wave by, crying how bright
Their frail deeds might have danced in a green bay,
Rage, rage against the dying of the light.

Wild men who caught and sang the sun in flight,
And learn, too late, they grieved it on its way,
Do not go gentle into that good night.

Grave men, near death, who see with blinding sight
Blind eyes could blaze like meteors and be gay,
Rage, rage against the dying of the light.

And you, my father, there on the sad height,
Curse, bless, me now with your fierce tears, I pray.
Do not go gentle into that good night.
Rage, rage against the dying of the light.

Table of Contents

Verse for a Certain Dog
by Dorothy Parker

Such glorious faith as fills your limpid eyes,
Dear little friend of mine, I never knew.
All-innocent are you, and yet all-wise.
(For Heaven's sake, stop worrying that shoe!)

You look about, and all you see is fair;
This mighty globe was made for you alone.
Of all the thunderous ages, you're the heir.
(Get off the pillow with that dirty bone!)

A skeptic world you face with steady gaze;
High in young pride you hold your noble head,
Gayly you meet the rush of roaring days.
(Must you eat puppy biscuit on the bed?)
Lancelike your courage, gleaming swift and strong,
Yours the white rapture of a winged soul,
Yours is a spirit like a Mayday song.
(God help you, if you break the goldfish bowl!)

"Whatever is, is good" - your gracious creed.
You wear your joy of living like a crown.
Love lights your simplest act, your every deed.
(Drop it, I tell you- put that kitten down!)
You are God's kindliest gift of all - a friend.
Your shining loyalty unflecked by doubt,
You ask but leave to follow to the end.
(Couldn't you wait until I took you out?)

Sasha Re-painted by Shelly Baxter
Photograph by Shelly Baxter

Catherine a C III Sasha Studio Doll by Sasha Morgenthaler in 1961
Photograph by Janet Myhill Dabbs
Knit by Janet Myhill Dabbs from a Knitting Pattern by Susanna Lewis

Stopping by Woods on a Snowy Evening
by Robert Frost

Whose woods these are I think I know.
His house is in the village though;
He will not see me stopping here
To watch his woods fill up with snow.

My little horse must think it queer
To stop without a farmhouse near
Between the woods and frozen lake
The darkest evening of the year.

He gives his harness bells a shake
To ask if there is some mistake.
The only other sound's the sweep
Of easy wind and downy flake.

The woods are lovely, dark and deep,
But I have promises to keep,
And miles to go before I sleep,
And miles to go before I sleep.

She Walks in Beauty
by Lord Byron (George Gordon)

She walks in beauty, like the night
Of cloudless climes and starry skies;
And all that's best of dark and bright
Meet in her aspect and her eyes;
Thus mellowed to that tender light
Which heaven to gaudy day denies.

One shade the more, one ray the less,
Had half impaired the nameless grace
Which waves in every raven tress,
Or softly lightens o'er her face;
Where thoughts serenely sweet express,
How pure, how dear their dwelling-place.

And on that cheek, and o'er that brow,
So soft, so calm, yet eloquent,
The smiles that win, the tints that glow,
But tell of days in goodness spent,
A mind at peace with all below,
A heart whose love is innocent!

Algerian Girl
Hand Painted Frido prototype by Sasha Morgenthaler
From the Collection of Brenda Walton
Photograph by Shelly Baxter

Photograph of Tiger and Ferris, a Trendon
1967 no philtrum doll by Mary Righos

Macavity - The Mystery Cat
by T. S. Eliot

Macavity's a Mystery Cat: he's called the Hidden Paw—
For he's the master criminal who can defy the Law.
He's the bafflement of Scotland Yard, the Flying Squad's despair:
For when they reach the scene of crime—Macavity's not there!

Macavity, Macavity, there's no one like Macavity,
He's broken every human law, he breaks the law of gravity.
His powers of levitation would make a fakir stare,
And when you reach the scene of crime—Macavity's not there!
You may seek him in the basement, you may look up in the air—
But I tell you once and once again, Macavity's not there!

Macavity's a ginger cat, he's very tall and thin;
You would know him if you saw him, for his eyes are sunken in.
His brow is deeply lined with thought, his head is highly domed;
His coat is dusty from neglect, his whiskers are uncombed.
He sways his head from side to side, with movements like a snake;
And when you think he's half asleep, he's always wide awake.

Macavity, Macavity, there's no one like Macavity,
For he's a fiend in feline shape, a monster of depravity.
You may meet him in a by-street, you may see him in the square—
But when a crime's discovered, then Macavity's not there!

He's outwardly respectable. (They say he cheats at cards.)
And his footprints are not found in any file of Scotland Yard's
And when the larder's looted, or the jewel-case is rifled,
Or when the milk is missing, or another Peke's been stifled,
Or the greenhouse glass is broken, and the trellis past repair
Ay, there's the wonder of the thing! Macavity's not there!

And when the Foreign Office find a Treaty's gone astray,
Or the Admiralty lose some plans and drawings by the way,
There may be a scrap of paper in the hall or on the stair—
But it's useless to investigate—Macavity's not there!
And when the loss has been disclosed, the Secret Service say:
It must have been Macavity!—but he's a mile away.
You'll be sure to find him resting, or a-licking of his thumb;
Or engaged in doing complicated long division sums.

Macavity, Macavity, there's no one like Macavity,
There never was a Cat of such deceitfulness and suavity.
He always has an alibi, and one or two to spare:
At whatever time the deed took place—
MACAVITY WASN'T THERE !
And they say that all the Cats whose wicked deeds are widely known
(I might mention Mungojerrie, I might mention Griddlebone)
Are nothing more than agents for the Cat who all the time
Just controls their operations: the Napoleon of Crime!

Sonnet XXV
Let those who are in favour with the stars
by William Shakespeare

Let those who are in favour with their stars
Of public honour and proud titles boast,
Whilst I, whom fortune of such triumph bars,
Unlook'd for joy in that I honour most.
Great princes' favourites their fair leaves spread
But as the marigold at the sun's eye,
And in themselves their pride lies buried,
For at a frown they in their glory die.
The painful warrior famoused for fight,
After a thousand victories once foil'd,
Is from the book of honour razed quite,
And all the rest forgot for which he toil'd:
Then happy I, that love and am beloved
Where I may not remove nor be removed.

Kipper and Molly as The Prince of Wales
Outfit knitted by Susanna Lewis
Photograph by Susanna Lewis

Ripe Plums are Falling
by Confucius
From the Chinese Book of Songs

ripe plums are falling
now there are only five
may a fine lover come for me
while there is still time

ripe plums are falling
now there are only three
may a fine lover come for me
while there is still time

ripe plums are falling
i gather them in a shallow basket
may a fine lover come for me
tell me his name

Photograph by Kendal Hackney
Sasha Doll Re-painted by Janet Myhill Dabbs

Photograph by Tatyana Petrova

Sail Away
by Rabindranath Tagore

Early in the day it was whispered that we should
sail in a boat,
only thou and I, and never a soul in the world
would know of this our pilgrimage
to no country and to no end.

In that shoreless ocean,
at thy silently listening smile my songs
would swell in melodies,
free as waves, free from all bondage of words.

Is the time not come yet?
Are there works still to do?
Lo, the evening has come down upon the shore
and in the fading light the seabirds come flying to
their nests.

Who knows when the chains will be off,
and the boat, like the last glimmer of sunset,
vanish into the night?

Come Home!
by Mary Elizabeth Coleridge

When wintry winds are no more heard,
And joy's in every bosom,
When summer sings in every bird,
And shines in every blossom,
When happy twilight hours are long,
Come home, my love, and think no wrong!

When berries gleam above the stream
And half the fields are yellow,
Come back to me, my joyous dream,
The world hath not thy fellow!
And I will make thee Queen among
The Queens of summer and of song

One of Kendal's Brood returns to the original
Trendon factory in Stockport, Greater Manchester.
Photograph by Kendal Hackney.

Sonnet CXXVIII
How oft, when thou, my music, music play'st
by William Shakespeare

How oft, when thou, my music, music play'st,
Upon that blessed wood whose motion sounds
With thy sweet fingers, when thou gently sway'st
The wiry concord that mine ear confounds,
Do I envy those jacks that nimble leap
To kiss the tender inward of thy hand,
Whilst my poor lips, which should that harvest reap,
At the wood's boldness by thee blushing stand!
To be so tickled, they would change their state
And situation with those dancing chips,
O'er whom thy fingers walk with gentle gait,
Making dead wood more blest than living lips.
Since saucy jacks so happy are in this,
Give them thy fingers, me thy lips to kiss.

Sasha Pintucks, Limited edition doll from 1982.
Photograph by Tyler Brunson O'Grady

Photograph by Shelly Baxter
1966 Graphic eyed No Philtrum

The Indian Gipsy
by Sarojini Naidu

In tattered robes that hoard a glittering trace
Of bygone colours, broidered to the knee,
Behold her, daughter of a wandering race,
Tameless, with the bold falcon's agile grace,
And the lithe tiger's sinuous majesty.

With frugal skill her simple wants she tends,
She folds her tawny heifers and her sheep
On lonely meadows when the daylight ends,
Ere the quick night upon her flock descends
Like a black panther from the caves of sleep.

Time's river winds in foaming centuries
Its changing, swift, irrevocable course
To far off and incalculable seas;
She is twin-born with primal mysteries,
And drinks of life at Time's forgotten source

The Road Not Taken
by Robert Frost

Two roads diverged in a yellow wood,
And sorry I could not travel both
And be one traveler, long I stood
And looked down one as far as I could
To where it bent in the undergrowth;

Then took the other, as just as fair,
And having perhaps the better claim,
Because it was grassy and wanted wear;
Though as for that the passing there
Had worn them really about the same,

And both that morning equally lay
In leaves no step had trodden black.
Oh, I kept the first for another day!
Yet knowing how way leads on to way,
I doubted if I should ever come back.

I shall be telling this with a sigh
Somewhere ages and ages hence:
Two roads diverged in a wood, and I—
I took the one less traveled by,
And that has made all the difference.

Re-painted and Re-wig by Shelly Baxter
Photograph by Shelly Baxter

In Mrs. Tilscher's Class
by Carol Ann Duffy

You could travel up the Blue Nile
with your finger, tracing the route
while Mrs Tilscher chanted the scenery.
Tana. Ethiopia. Khartoum. Aswân.
That for an hour, then a skittle of milk
and the chalky Pyramids rubbed into dust.
A window opened with a long pole.
The laugh of a bell swung by a running child.
This was better than home. Enthralling books.
The classroom glowed like a sweet shop.
Sugar paper. Coloured shapes. Brady and Hindley
faded, like the faint, uneasy smudge of a mistake.
Mrs Tilscher loved you. Some mornings, you found
she'd left a good gold star by your name.
The scent of a pencil slowly, carefully, shaved.
A xylophone's nonsense heard from another form.
Over the Easter term, the inky tadpoles changed
from commas into exclamation marks. Three frogs
hopped in the playground, freed by a dunce,
followed by a line of kids, jumping and croaking
away from the lunch queue. A rough boy
told you how you were born. You kicked him, but
stared at your parents, appalled, when you got back
home.
That feverish July, the air tasted of electricity.
A tangible alarm made you always untidy, hot,
fractious under the heavy, sexy sky. You asked her
how you were born and Mrs Tilscher smiled,
then turned away. Reports were handed out.

You ran through the gates, impatient to be grown,
as the sky split open into a thunderstorm.

Sasha Pintucks, Limited edition doll from 1982.
Photograph by Tyler Brunson O'Grady

Sasha Re-root by Tatyana Petrova
Photograph by Tatyana Petrova

As I cam down by yon castle wa',
by Robert Burns

As I cam down by yon castle wa',
And in by yon garden green,
O there I spied a bony bony lass,
But the flower-borders were us between.

A bony bony lassie she was,
As ever mine eyes did see:
O five hundred pounds would I give,
For to have such a pretty bride as thee.

To have such a pretty bride as me,
Young man ye are sairly mista'en;
Tho' ye were king o' fair Scotland,
I wad disdain to be you queen.

Talk not so very high, bony lass,
O talk not so very, very high:
The man at the fair that wad sell,
He maun learn at the man that wad buy.

I trust to climb a far higher tree,
And herry a far richer nest:
Tak this advice o' me, bony lass,
Humility wad set thee best.

Ode To The Lemon
by Pablo Neruda

From blossoms released by the moonlight,
from an aroma of exasperated love,
steeped in fragrance,
yellowness drifted from the lemon tree,
and from its plantarium
lemons descended to the earth.

Tender yield!
The coasts, the markets glowed with light,

With unrefined gold;
we opened two halves of a miracle,
congealed acid trickled from the
Hemispheres of a star,
the most intense liqueur of nature,
unique, vivid, concentrated,
born of the cool, fresh lemon, of its fragrant house,
its acid, secret symmetry.

Knives sliced a small cathedral in the lemon,
the concealed apse, opened, revealed acid stained glass,
drops oozed topaz, altars, cool architecture.

So, when you hold the hemisphere
of a cut lemon above your plate,
you spill a universe of gold, a yellow goblet of miracles,
a fragrant nipple of the earth's breast,
a ray of light that was made fruit,
the minute fire of a planet.

2ⁿᵈ edition Götz Sasha and Toddler.
Photographs by Tyler Brunson O'Grady

Mallory, a CIII Studio Doll by Sasha Morgenthaler
from 1969
Photograph by Janet Myhill Dabbs

I started Early - Took my Dog
by Emily Dickinson

I started Early - Took my Dog -
And visited the Sea -
The Mermaids in the Basement
Came out to look at me -

And Frigates - in the Upper Floor
Extended Hempen Hands -
Presuming Me to be a Mouse -
Aground - opon the Sands -

But no Man moved Me - till the Tide
Went past my simple Shoe -
And past my Apron - and my Belt
And past my Boddice - too -

And made as He would eat me up -
As wholly as a Dew
Opon a Dandelion's Sleeve -
And then - I started - too -

And He - He followed - close behind -
I felt His Silver Heel
Opon my Ancle - Then My Shoes
Would overflow with Pearl -

Until We met the Solid Town -
No One He seemed to know -
And bowing - with a Mighty look -
At me - The Sea withdrew -

Photograph by Kendal Hackney

Keepsake Mill
By Robert Louis Stevenson

Over the borders, a sin without pardon,
    Breaking the branches and crawling below,
Out through the breach in the wall of the garden,
    Down by the banks of the river we go.

Here is a mill with the humming of thunder,
    Here is the weir with the wonder of foam,
Here is the sluice with the race running under—
    Marvellous places, though handy to home!

Sounds of the village grow stiller and stiller,
    Stiller the note of the birds on the hill;
Dusty and dim are the eyes of the miller,
    Deaf are his ears with the moil of the mill.

Years may go by, and the wheel in the river
    Wheel as it wheels for us, children, to-day,
Wheel and keep roaring and foaming for ever
    Long after all of the boys are away.

Home for the Indies and home from the ocean,
    Heroes and soldiers we all will come home;
Still we shall find the old mill wheel in motion,
    Turning and churning that river to foam.

You with the bean that I gave when we quarrelled,
    I with your marble of Saturday last,
Honoured and old and all gaily apparelled,
    Here we shall meet and remember the past.

*Sleeping Sasha Repainted and Posable Body Replacement
by Janet Myhill Dabbs*
Photograph by Janet Myhill Dabbs

A Child's Thought
By Robert Louis Stevenson

At seven, when I go to bed,
I find such pictures in my head:
Castles with dragons prowling round,
Gardens where magic fruits are found;
Fair ladies prisoned in a tower,
Or lost in an enchanted bower;
While **gallant** horsemen ride by streams
That border all this land of dreams
I find, so clearly in my head
At seven, when I go to bed.

At seven, when I wake again,
The magic land I seek in vain;
A chair stands where the castle frowned,
The carpet hides the garden ground,
No fairies trip across the floor,
Boots, and not horsemen, flank the door,
And where the blue streams rippling ran
Is now a bath and water-can;
I seek the magic land in vain
At seven, when I wake again.

When I have fears that I may cease to be
by John Keats

When I have fears that I may cease to be
Before my pen has gleaned my teeming brain,
Before high-pilèd books, in charactery,
Hold like rich garners the full ripened grain;
When I behold, upon the night's starred face,
Huge cloudy symbols of a high romance,
And think that I may never live to trace
Their shadows with the magic hand of chance;
And when I feel, fair creature of an hour,
That I shall never look upon thee more,
Never have relish in the faery power
Of unreflecting love—then on the shore
Of the wide world I stand alone, and think
Till love and fame to nothingness do sink.

"Benny", an early BII Studio Doll
Photograph by Cathy Himmel

1966 No Philtrum Sasha with developmental eyes
Photograph by Leslie Anne Hendra

Into my heart an air that kills
by A. E. Housman

Into my heart an air that kills
From yon far country blows;
What are those blue remembered hills,
What spires, what farms are those?
That is the land of lost content,
I see it shining plain,
The happy highways where I went
And cannot come again.

Reflections on a Gift of Watermelon Pickle Received from a Friend Called Felicity
by John Tobias

During that summer
When unicorns were still possible;
When the purpose of knees
Was to be skinned'
When shiny horse chestnuts
    (hollowed out fitted with straws crammed with tobacco
stolen from butts in family ashtrays)

Were puffed in green lizard silence
While straddling thick branches
Far above and away
From the softening effects of civilization;

During that summer—
Which may never have been at all;
But which has become more real
Than the one that was—
Watermelons ruled.

Thick pink imperial slices
Melting frigidly on sun-parched tongues
Dribbling from chins;
Leaving the best part,
The black bullet seeds,
To be spit out in rapid fire
Against the wall
Against the wind
Against each other;
And when the ammunition was spent,
There was always another bite:
It was a summer of limitless bites,
Of hungers quickly felt
And quickly forgotten
With the next careless gorging.

The bites are fewer now.
Each one is savoured lingeringly,
Swallowed reluctantly.

But in a jar put up by Felicity,
The summer which never maybe was
Has been captured and preserved.
And when we unscrew the lid
And slice off a piece
And let it linger on our tongue:
Unicorns become possible again.

Sasha Repainted by Shelly Baxter, Re-rooted by Alison Parnell
Photo by Shelly Baxter

How to Eat a Poem
by Eve Merriam

Don't be polite.
Bite in,
Pick it up with your fingers and lick the juice that
may run down your chin.
It is ready and ripe now, whenever you are.

You do not need a knife or fork or spoon
or plate or napkin or tablecloth.

For there is no core
or stem
or rind
or pit
or seed
or skin
to throw away.

Cherry Blossom Haiku

Moon at twilight
a cluster of petals falling
from the cherry tree
    - Masaoka Shiki

Wind blows
they scatter and it dies
fallen petals
    - Yosa Buson

cherry blossom petals
blown by the spring breeze against
the undried wall
      Masaoka Shiki

Petals falling
unable to resist
the moonlight
      Yosa Buson

cherry blossoms scatter–
snap! the buck's antlers
come off
      Kobayashi Issa

without regret
they fall and scatter...
cherry blossoms
      Kobayashi Issa

Analise BIII Studio Doll by Sasha Morgenthaler
Photo by Mary Righos

Two 1968 Single Fringe Sasha Dolls
by Frido (later Trendon), England
Photograph by Liss Camber

One Sister have I in our house
by Emily Dickinson

One Sister have I in our house -
And one a hedge away.
There's only one recorded,
But both belong to me.

One came the way that I came -
And wore my past year's gown -
The other as a bird her nest,
Builded our hearts among.

She did not sing as we did -
It was a different tune   -
Herself to her a Music
As Bumble-bee of June.

Today is far from Childhood -
But up and down the hills
I held her hand the tighter -
Which shortened all the miles -

And still her hum
The years among,
Deceives the Butterfly;
Still in her Eye
The Violets lie
Mouldered this many May.

I spilt the dew -
But took the morn, -
I chose this single star
From out the wide night's numbers -
Sue - forevermore!

Those Winter Sundays
by Robert Hayden

Sundays too my father got up early
and put his clothes on in the blueblack cold,
then with cracked hands that ached
from labor in the weekday weather made
banked fires blaze. No one ever thanked him.

I'd wake and hear the cold splintering, breaking.
When the rooms were warm, he'd call,
and slowly I would rise and dress,
fearing the chronic angers of that house,

Speaking indifferently to him,
who had driven out the cold
and polished my good shoes as well.
What did I know, what did I know
of love's austere and lonely offices?

1968 Single Fringe Sasha Doll
by Frido (later Trendon), England
Photograph by Vicky Chapman

Golden Slumbers Kiss Your Eyes
by Thomas Dekker

Golden slumbers kiss your eyes,
Smiles awake you when you rise ;
Sleep, pretty wantons, do not cry,
And I will sing a lullaby,

Rock them, rock them, lullaby.
Care is heavy, therefore sleep you,
You are care, and care must keep you;

Sleep, pretty wantons, do not cry,
And I will sing a lullaby,
Rock them, rock them, lullaby.

Photograph by JoAnn Staricha

i carry your heart with me
by E. E. Cummings

i carry your heart with me (i carry it in
my heart) i am never without it (anywhere
i go you go, my dear; and whatever is done
by only me is your doing, my darling)
                                        i fear
no fate (for you are my fate, my sweet) i want
no world (for beautiful you are my world, my true)
and it's you are whatever a moon has always meant
and whatever a sun will always sing is you

here is the deepest secret nobody knows
(here is the root of the root and the bud of the bud
and the sky of the sky of a tree called life; which grows
higher than soul can hope or mind can hide)
and this is the wonder that's keeping the stars apart

i carry your heart (i carry it in my heart)

Prototype "Alice" Sasha Doll
Hand painted Frido by Sasha Morgenthaler
Courtesy of Brenda Walton
Photographed by Shelly Baxter

The Moon was but a Chin of Gold
By Emily Dickinson

The Moon was but a Chin of Gold
A Night or two ago—
And now she turns Her perfect Face
Upon the World below—

Her Forehead is of Amplest Blonde—
Her Cheek—a Beryl hewn—
Her Eye unto the Summer Dew
The likest I have known—

Her Lips of Amber never part—
But what must be the smile
Upon Her Friend she could confer
Were such Her Silver Will—

And what a privilege to be
But the remotest Star—
For Certainty She take Her Way
Beside Your Palace Door—

Photo by Fiona Hinchcliffe

The House at Pooh Corner
by A. A. Milne

"I think we dream so we don't have to be apart for so
long. If we're in each other's dreams, we can be
together all the time."

Then, suddenly again, Christopher Robin, who was
still looking at the world, with his chin in his hands,
called out "Pooh!"

"Yes?" said Pooh.

"When I'm----when----Pooh!"

"Yes, Christopher Robin?"

"I'm not going to do Nothing any more."

"Never again?"

"Well, not so much. They don't let you."

Pooh waited for him to go on, but he was silent
again

"Yes, Christopher Robin?" said Pooh helpfully.

"Pooh, when I'm----you know----when I'm not doing
nothing, will you come up here sometimes?"

"Just Me?"

"Yes, Pooh."

"Will you be here too?"

"Yes, Pooh, I will be, really. I promise I will be,
Pooh."

"That's good," said Pooh.

"Pooh, promise you won't forget about me, ever.
Not even when I'm a hundred."

Pooh thought for a little while.

"How old shall I be then?"

"Ninety-nine."

Pooh nodded. "I promise," he said.

Still with his eyes on the world Christopher Robin put
out a hand and felt for Pooh's paw.

"Pooh," said Christopher Robin earnestly, "If I----if I'm not quite----" he stopped and tried again---- "Pooh whatever happens, you will understand, won't you?"

"Understand what?"

"Oh, nothing." He laughed and jumped to his feet. "Come on!"

"Where?" said Pooh.

"Anywhere," said Christopher Robin.

So they went off together. But wherever they go, and whatever happens to them on the way, in that enchanted place on top of the Forest, a little boy and his Bear will always be playing.

2nd Edition Götz Sasha
Photograph by Tyler Brunson O'Grady

"Velvet" a Limited Edition Sasha from 1981
Mr. Fox knit ensemble by Susan O'Brien
Photograph by Susan O'Brien

The Thought-Fox
by Ted Hughes

I imagine this midnight moment's forest:
Something else is alive
Beside the clock's loneliness
And this blank page where my fingers move.

Through the window I see no star:
Something more near
Though deeper within darkness
Is entering the loneliness:

Cold, delicately as the dark snow
A fox's nose touches twig, leaf;
Two eyes serve a movement, that now
And again now, and now, and now

Sets neat prints into the snow
Between trees, and warily a lame
Shadow lags by stump and in hollow
Of a body that is bold to come

Across clearings, an eye,
A widening deepening greenness,
Brilliantly, concentratedly,
Coming about its own business

Till, with a sudden sharp hot stink of fox
It enters the dark hole of the head.
The window is starless still; the clock ticks,
The page is printed.

Alone
by Maya Angelou

Lying, thinking last night
How to find my soul a home
Where water is not thirsty
And bread loaf is not stone
I came up with one thing
And I don't believe I'm wrong
That nobody, But nobody
Can make it out here alone.

Alone, all alone
Nobody, but nobody
Can make it out here alone.

There are some millionaires
Their wives run round like banshees
Their children sing the blues
They've got expensive doctors
To cure their hearts of stone.
But nobody. No, nobody
Can make it out here alone.

Alone, all alone
Nobody, but nobody
Can make it out here alone.

Now if you listen closely
I'll tell you what I know
Storm clouds are gathering
The wind is gonna blow
The race of man is suffering
And I can hear the moan,

'Cause nobody, But nobody
Can make it out here alone.

Alone, all alone
Nobody, but nobody
Can make it out here alone.

Lindiwee Painted and Braided by Janet Myhill Dabbs
Outfit by Anna Page
Photograph by Janet Myhill Dabbs

Invictus
by William Ernest Henley

Out of the night that covers me,
Black as the pit from pole to pole,
I thank whatever gods may be
For my unconquerable soul.

In the fell clutch of circumstance
I have not winced nor cried aloud.
Under the bludgeonings of chance
My head is bloody, but unbowed.

Beyond this place of wrath and tears
Looms but the Horror of the shade,
And yet the menace of the years
Finds and shall find me unafraid.

It matters not how strait the gate,
How charged with punishments the scroll,
I am the master of my fate,
I am the captain of my soul.

BIII Studio Doll
Photograph by Cathy Himmel

Heidenröslein (The Rose Among the Heather)
by Johann Wolfgang von Goethe

Grew a baby rosebud rare,
Lonely—'mong the heather;
Morning was not half so fair,
One looked long who, lingering there,
Fain had looked forever.
Dainty, wayward, crimson rose;
Rosebud 'mong the heather;
"Sweet, I'll steal thee, ay or no!"
Quoth he, from the heather.
"Then I'll prick thee," laughed she low,
Heedless, heartless—even so,
"Thou'll think on me ever."
Rosebud, rosebud; red, red rose;
Rosebud 'mong the heather.
Willful wooers are not slow,
Rosebud's o'er the heather.
Thorns can wound till life-drops flow;
In two hearts a weary woe
Woke to slumber never.
Rosebud, rosebud; red, red rose;
Rosebud 'mong the heather.

Prototype "Brunette" Sasha Doll
Hand painted Frido by Sasha Morgenthaler
Courtesy of Brenda Walton
Photographed by Shelly Baxter

Composed upon Westminster Bridge
by William Wordsworth

Earth has not anything to show more fair:
Dull would he be of soul who could pass by
A sight so touching in its majesty:

This City now doth, like a garment, wear
The beauty of the morning: silent, bare,
Ships, towers, domes, theatres, and temples lie
Open unto the fields, and to the sky;

All bright and glittering in the smokeless air.
Never did sun more beautifully steep
In his first splendour, valley, rock, or hill;

Ne'er saw I, never felt, a calm so deep!
The river glideth at his own sweet will:
Dear God! the very houses seem asleep;
And all that mighty heart is lying still!

1966 Graphic Eye NP Frido Sasha
2014 Sasha Festival souvenir dress made by Marti Sanders Murphy.
Go-go boots were made by Lisa Sasha.
Photographed by Cathy Himmel

"Robin" , a 1st production Saucer Eyed, No Navel
Götz from 1969/1970
Photo by Cathy Himmel

Sonnet XVIII
Shall I compare thee to a summer's day?
by William Shakespeare

I compare thee to a summer's day?
Thou art more lovely and more temperate:

Rough winds do shake the darling buds of May,
And summer's lease hath all too short a date:

Sometime too hot the eye of heaven shines,
And often is his gold complexion dimmed,
And every fair from fair sometime declines,
By chance, or nature's changing course untrimmed:

But thy eternal summer shall not fade,
Nor lose possession of that fair thou ow'st,
Nor shall death brag thou wander'st in his shade,
When in eternal lines to time thou grow'st,
So long as men can breathe, or eyes can see,
So long lives this, and this gives life to thee.

Friendship
By Henry David Thoreau

I think a while of Love, and while I think,
Love is to me a world,
Sole meat and sweetest drink,
And close connecting link
Tween heaven and earth.
I only know it is, not how or why,
My greatest happiness; however hard I try,
Not if I were to die,
Can I explain.
I fain would ask my friend how it can be,
But when the time arrives,
Then Love is more lovely, than anything to me,
And so I'm dumb.
For if the truth were known, Love cannot speak,
But only thinks and does;
Though surely out 'twill leak
Without the help of Greek,
Or any tongue.
A man may love the truth and practise it,
Beauty he may admire, and goodness not omit,
As much as may befit to reverence.
But only when these three together meet,
As they always incline,
And make one soul the seat,
And favorite retreat,
Of loveliness;
When under kindred shape, like loves and hates
And a kindred nature, proclaim us to be mates,
Exposed to equal fates eternally;
And each may other help, and service do,
Drawing Love's bands more tight,

Service he ne'er shall rue
While one and one make two,
And two are one;
In such case only doth man fully prove
Fully as man can do,
What power there is in Love
His inmost soul to move resistlessly.
Two sturdy oaks I mean, which side by side,
Withstand the winter's storm,
And spite of wind and tide,
Grow up the meadow's pride,
For both are strong
Above they barely touch, but undermined
Down to their deepest source,
Admiring you shall find
Their roots are intertwined insep'rably.

Repainted "Gertie" sisters by Janet Myhill Dabbs
Photograph by Kendal Hackney

If
by Rudyard Kipling

If you can keep your head when all about you
    Are losing theirs and blaming it on you,
If you can trust yourself when all men doubt you,
    But make allowance for their doubting too;
If you can wait and not be tired by waiting,
    Or being lied about, don't deal in lies,
Or being hated, don't give way to hating,
    And yet don't look too good, nor talk too wise:

If you can dream—and not make dreams your master;
    If you can think—and not make thoughts your aim;
If you can meet with Triumph and Disaster
    And treat those two impostors just the same;
If you can bear to hear the truth you've spoken
    Twisted by knaves to make a trap for fools,
Or watch the things you gave your life to, broken,
    And stoop and build 'em up with worn-out tools:

If you can make one heap of all your winnings
    And risk it on one turn of pitch-and-toss,
And lose, and start again at your beginnings
    And never breathe a word about your loss;
If you can force your heart and nerve and sinew
    To serve your turn long after they are gone,
And so hold on when there is nothing in you
    Except the Will which says to them: 'Hold on!'

If you can talk with crowds and keep your virtue,
    Or walk with Kings—nor lose the common touch,
If neither foes nor loving friends can hurt you,
    If all men count with you, but none too much;

If you can fill the unforgiving minute
    With sixty seconds' worth of distance run,
Yours is the Earth and everything that's in it,
    And—which is more—you'll be a Man, my son!

"Linzer" A CIII Studio Doll
Illustration by Cathy Himmel

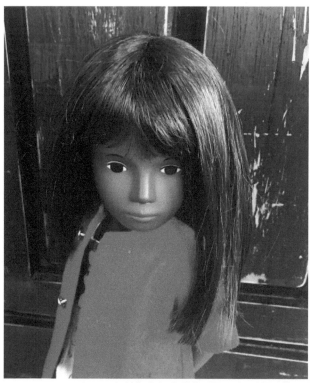

A wigged Caleb doll by Trendon, England
Photo by Cathy Himmel

Still, I Rise
by Maya Angelou

You may write me down in history
With your bitter, twisted lies,
You may tread me in the very dirt
But still, like dust, I'll rise.

Does my sassiness upset you?
Why are you beset with gloom?
'Cause I walk like I've got oil wells
Pumping in my living room.
Just like moons and like suns,

With the certainty of tides,
Just like hopes springing high, still I'll rise.

Did you want to see me broken?
Bowed head and lowered eyes?
Shoulders falling down like teardrops.
Weakened by my soulful cries.

Does my haughtiness offend you?
Don't you take it awful hard
'Cause I laugh like I've got gold mines
Diggin' in my own back yard.

You may shoot me with your words,
You may cut me with your eyes,
You may kill me with your hatefulness,
But still, like air, I'll rise.

Does my sexiness upset you?
Does it come as a surprise
That I dance like I've got diamonds
At the meeting of my thighs?

Out of the huts of history's shame I rise
Up from a past that's rooted in pain I rise
I'm a black ocean, leaping and wide,
Welling and swelling I bear in the tide.
Leaving behind nights of terror and fear I rise
Into a daybreak that's wondrously clear I rise
Bringing the gifts that my ancestors gave,
I am the dream and the hope of the slave.
I rise
I rise
I rise.

Desiderata
by Max Ehrmann

Go placidly amid the noise and haste,
and remember what peace there may be in silence.
As far as possible without surrender
be on good terms with all persons.
Speak your truth quietly and clearly;
and listen to others,
even the dull and the ignorant;
they too have their story.
Avoid loud and aggressive persons,
they are vexations to the spirit.
If you compare yourself with others,
you may become vain and bitter;
for always there will be greater and lesser persons than
yourself.
Enjoy your achievements as well as your plans.
Keep interested in your own career, however humble;
it is a real possession in the changing fortunes of time.
Exercise caution in your business affairs;
for the world is full of trickery.
But let this not blind you to what virtue there is;
many persons strive for high ideals;
and everywhere life is full of heroism.
Be yourself.
Especially, do not feign affection.
Neither be cynical about love;
for in the face of all aridity and disenchantment
it is as perennial as the grass.
Take kindly the counsel of the years,
gracefully surrendering the things of youth.
Nurture strength of spirit to shield you in sudden
misfortune.

But do not distress yourself with dark imaginings.
Many fears are born of fatigue and loneliness.
Beyond a wholesome discipline,
be gentle with yourself.
You are a child of the universe,
no less than the trees and the stars;
you have a right to be here.
And whether or not it is clear to you,
no doubt the universe is unfolding as it should.
Therefore be at peace with God,
whatever you conceive Him to be,
and whatever your labors and aspirations,
in the noisy confusion of life keep peace with your soul.
With all its sham, drudgery, and broken dreams,
it is still a beautiful world.
Be cheerful. Strive to be happy.

1969 Blonde Frido Sasha repainted by Shelly Baxter
Photographed by Liss Camber

Photograph by Michele Balli Tasabia

On the Sea
By John Keats

It keeps eternal whisperings around
Desolate shores, and with its mighty swell
Gluts twice ten thousand caverns, till the spell
Of Hecate leaves them their old shadowy sound.
Often 'tis in such gentle temper found,
That scarcely will the very smallest shell
Be moved for days from where it sometime fell,
When last the winds of heaven were unbound.
O ye! who have your eyeballs vexed and tired,
Feast them upon the wideness of the Sea;
O ye! whose ears are dinn'd with uproar rude,
Or fed too much with cloying melody, –
Sit ye near some old cavern's mouth, and brood
Until ye start, as if the sea-nymphs quired!

Fern Hill
By Dylan Thomas

Now as I was young and easy under the apple boughs
About the lilting house and happy as the grass was green,
The night above the dingle starry,
Time let me hail and climb
Golden in the heydays of his eyes,
And honoured among wagons I was prince of the apple towns
And once below a time I lordly had the trees and leaves
Trail with daisies and barley
Down the rivers of the windfall light.
And as I was green and carefree, famous among the barns
About the happy yard and singing as the farm was home,
In the sun that is young once only, time let me play and be
Golden in the mercy of his means,
And green and golden I was huntsman and herdsman, the calves
Sang to my horn, the foxes on the hills barked clear and cold,
And the sabbath rang slowly in the pebbles of the holy streams.
All the sun long it was running, it was lovely, the hay
Fields high as the house, the tunes from the chimneys, it was air
And playing, lovely and watery and fire green as grass.
And nightly under the simple stars
As I rode to sleep the owls were bearing the farm away,
All the moon long I heard, blessed among stables, the nightjars
Flying with the ricks, and the horses flashing into the dark.
And then to awake, and the farm, like a wanderer white
With the dew, come back, the cock on his shoulder: it was all
Shining, it was Adam and maiden, the sky gathered again
And the sun grew round that very day.
So it must have been after the birth of the simple light
In the first, spinning place, the spellbound horses walking warm
Out of the whinnying green stable on to the fields of praise.

And honoured among foxes and pheasants by the gay house
Under the new made clouds and happy as the heart was long,
In the sun born over and over, I ran my heedless ways,
My wishes raced through the house high hay
And nothing I cared, at my sky blue trades, that time allows
In all his tuneful turning so few and such morning songs
Before the children green and golden follow him out of grace,
Nothing I cared, in the lamb white days, that time would take me
Up to the swallow thronged loft by the shadow of my hand,
In the moon that is always rising, nor that riding to sleep
I should hear him fly with the high fields
And wake to the farm forever fled from the childless land.
Oh as I was young and easy in the mercy of his means,
Time held me green and dying
Though I sang in my chains like the sea.

"Gertie Clarisse" *Repainted and rewigged by Janet Myhill Dabbs*
Photo by Kendal Hackney

The End of the Rope
by Margaret Nickerson Martin

When you've lost every vestige of hope
And you think you are beaten and done,

When you've come to the end of your rope,
Tie a knot in the end and hang on.
Have courage; for here is the dope;

When you stand with your back to the wall,
Though you've come to the end of your rope
Tie a knot in the end and hang on.

Don't admit that life's getting your goat
When your friends seem to all disappear,
When you've come to the end of your rope,
Tie a knot in the end and hang on.

CIII Studio Doll Number 210 from 1969 by Sasha Morgenthaler
Photo by Janet Myhill Dabbs

As Imperceptibly as Grief
by Emily Dickinson

As imperceptibly as Grief
The Summer lapsed away –
Too imperceptible at last
To seem like Perfidy –
A Quietness distilled
As Twilight long begun,
Or Nature spending with herself
Sequestered Afternoon –
The Dusk drew earlier in –
The Morning foreign shone –
A courteous, yet harrowing Grace,
As Guest, that would be gone –
And thus, without a Wing
Or service of a Keel
Our Summer made her light escape
Into the Beautiful.

Prototype "Autumn" Sasha Doll
Hand painted Frido by Sasha Morgenthaler
Courtesy of Brenda Walton
Photographed by Shelly Baxter

I Love to See the Summer Beaming Forth
by John Clare

I love to see the summer beaming forth
And white wool sack clouds sailing to the north
I love to see the wild flowers come again
And mare blobs stain with gold the meadow drain
And water lilies whiten on the floods
Where reed clumps rustle like a wind shook wood
Where from her hiding place the Moor Hen pushes
And seeks her flag nest floating in bull rushes
I like the willow leaning half way o'er
The clear deep lake to stand upon its shore
I love the hay grass when the flower head swings
To summer winds and insects happy wings
That sport about the meadow the bright day
And see bright beetles in the clear lake play

A No Philtrum Sasha by Frido (later Trendon), England
Photograph by Theresa O'Neill

Blackberry-Picking
By Seamus Heaney

Late August, given heavy rain and sun
For a full week, the blackberries would ripen.
At first, just one, a glossy purple clot
Among others, red, green, hard as a knot.
You ate that first one and its flesh was sweet
Like thickened wine: summer's blood was in it
Leaving stains upon the tongue and lust for
Picking. Then red ones inked up and that hunger
Sent us out with milk cans, pea tins, jam-pots
Where briars scratched and wet grass bleached our boots.
Round hayfields, cornfields and potato-drills
We trekked and picked until the cans were full
Until the tinkling bottom had been covered
With green ones, and on top big dark blobs burned
Like a plate of eyes. Our hands were peppered
With thorn pricks, our palms sticky as Bluebeard's.
We hoarded the fresh berries in the byre.
But when the bath was filled we found a fur,
A rat-grey fungus, glutting on our cache.
The juice was stinking too. Once off the bush
The fruit fermented, the sweet flesh would turn sour.
I always felt like crying. It wasn't fair
That all the lovely canfuls smelt of rot.
Each year I hoped they'd keep, knew they would not.

A No Philtrum Sasha by Frido (later Trendon), England
Photo by Jackie Rydstrom
Courtesy of Anita Fox

A 1966 Graphic Eyed, No Philtrum Sasha
by Frido (later Trendon), England
Photo by Julian Stanislaw Kalinowski

In the Person of Womankind
by Ben Jonson

Men, if you love us, play no more
The fools or tyrants with your friends,
To make us still sing o'er and o'er
Our own false praises, for your ends:
We have both wits and fancies too,
And, if we must, let's sing of you.

Nor do we doubt but that we can,
If we would search with care and pain,
Find some one good in some one man;
So going thorough all your strain,
We shall, at last, of parcels make
One good enough for a song's sake.

And as a cunning painter takes,
In any curious piece you see,
More pleasure while the thing he makes,
Than when 'tis made - why so will we.
And having pleased our art, we'll try
To make a new, and hang that by.

"Plum", a BIII Studio Doll by Sasha Morgenthaler
Photo by Cathy Himmel

This Is Just To Say
by William Carlos Williams

I have eaten
the plums
that were in
the icebox

and which
you were probably
saving
for breakfast

Forgive me
they were delicious
so sweet
and so cold

To Autumn
by John Keats

Season of mists and mellow fruitfulness,
Close bosom-friend of the maturing sun;
Conspiring with him how to load and bless
With fruit the vines that round the thatch-eves run;
To bend with apples the moss'd cottage-trees,
And fill all fruit with ripeness to the core;
To swell the gourd, and plump the hazel shells
With a sweet kernel; to set budding more,
And still more, later flowers for the bees,
Until they think warm days will never cease,
For summer has o'er-brimm'd their clammy cells.

Who hath not seen thee oft amid thy store?
Sometimes whoever seeks abroad may find
Thee sitting careless on a granary floor,
Thy hair soft-lifted by the winnowing wind;
Or on a half-reap'd furrow sound asleep,
Drows'd with the fume of poppies, while thy hook
Spares the next swath and all its twined flowers:
And sometimes like a gleaner thou dost keep
Steady thy laden head across a brook;
Or by a cyder-press, with patient look,
Thou watchest the last oozings hours by hours.

Where are the songs of spring? Ay, Where are they?
Think not of them, thou hast thy music too,—
While barred clouds bloom the soft-dying day,
And touch the stubble-plains with rosy hue;
Then in a wailful choir the small gnats mourn
Among the river sallows, borne aloft

Or sinking as the light wind lives or dies;
And full-grown lambs loud bleat from hilly bourn;
Hedge-crickets sing; and now with treble soft
The red-breast whistles from a garden-croft;
And gathering swallows twitter in the skies.

Outfits knitted by Janet Myhill Dabbs
Photo by Mary Righos

"Little Nellie", A BIII Studio Doll with her trunk of clothes.
Photo by Ginger Mullins

My Father's Trunk
By Raymond Roseliep

The soft grainy light of our attic opened my father's past a
little way. His trunk was a place where years were shut in
him like the leaves of a book whose title alone he displayed
I wondered if it was mostly about love, though other
strengths were there pressing a vision on my landscape. I
loved the hunters riding in coon-tail caps through the
ornamental path inside the lid—I knew by heart the clipping
how he bagged a timber wolf in some woods near Farley,
Iowa, and I sported the brass knuckles and dangled the
billyclub of his sheriff days, I aimed the elegant pistol at
spider targets—the topmost color in my first spectrum was
the green-pearl of the handle. Under the sulphur white
shirts with hard collars and their beautiful musty smell and
the old leather smell of razorstrap were keys to locks I never
could open; an oval locket, sealed tight as a dream, carried I
always thought my mother's image. I tried never to laugh at
the ohio matchbox with the sewing kit of his bachelor days,
and though it was hard to picture the big fingers threading a
needle, I once saw that hand lift a bluebell from its tower
and twirl it like a sparkler. The letter in the blue envelope he
had never opened bore a script daintier than my mother's
exquisite flourish, and when I left the blue flap sealed,
ordinary breathing avowed the silence but did not disturb it.

Counting-Out Rhyme
By Edna St. Vincent Millay

Silver bark of beech, and sallow
Bark of yellow birch and yellow
Twig of willow.

Stripe of green in moosewood maple,
Colour seen in leaf of apple,
Bark of popple.

Wood of popple pale as moonbeam,
Wood of oak for yoke and barn-beam,
Wood of hornbeam.

Silver bark of beech, and hollow
Stem of elder, tall and yellow
Twig of willow.

Various Götz Sasha Dolls from the 1960's
Outfits made by Janet Myhill Dabbs
Photo by Peggy Livingston

The Birch Tree
By James Russell Lowell

Rippling through thy branches goes the sunshine,
Among thy leaves that palpitate forever;
Ovid in thee a pining Nymph had prisoned,
The soul once of some tremulous inland river,
Quivering to tell her woe, but, ah! dumb, dumb forever!

While all the forest, witched with slumberous moonshine,
Holds up its leaves in happy, happy stillness,
Waiting the dew, with breath and pulse suspended,
I hear afar thy whispering, gleamy islands,
And track thee wakeful still amid the wide-hung silence.

On the brink of some wood-nestled lakelet,
Thy foliage, like the tresses of a Dryad,
Dripping round thy slim white stem, whose shadow
Slopes quivering down the water's dusky quiet,
Thou shrink'st as on her bath's edge would some startled Naiad.

Thou art the go-between of rustic lovers;
Thy white bark has their secrets in its keeping;
Reuben writes here the happy name of Patience,
And thy lithe boughs hang murmuring and weeping
Above her, as she steals the mystery from thy keeping.

Thou art to me like my beloved maiden,
So frankly coy, so full of trembly confidences;
Thy shadow scarce seems shade, thy pattering leaflets
Sprinkle their gathered sunshine o'er my senses,
And Nature gives me all her summer confidences.

Whether my heart with hope or sorrow tremble,
Thou sympathizest still; wild and unquiet,
I fling me down; thy ripple, like a river,
Flows valleyward, where calmness is, and by it
My heart is floated down into the land of quiet.

Photo and outfit hand-made by Vicky Chapman

The Retreat
By Henry Vaughn

Happy those early days! when I
Shined in my angel infancy.
Before I understood this place
Appointed for my second race,
Or taught my soul to fancy aught
But a white, celestial thought;
When yet I had not walked above
A mile or two from my first love,
And looking back, at that short space,
Could see a glimpse of His bright face;
When on some gilded cloud or flower
My gazing soul would dwell an hour,
And in those weaker glories spy
Some shadows of eternity;
Before I taught my tongue to wound
My conscience with a sinful sound,
Or had the black art to dispense
A several sin to every sense,
But felt through all this fleshly dress
Bright shoots of everlastingness.

O, how I long to travel back,
And tread again that ancient track!
That I might once more reach that plain
Where first I left my glorious train,
From whence th' enlightened spirit sees
That shady city of palm trees.

But, ah! my soul with too much stay
Is drunk, and staggers in the way.

Some men a forward motion love;
But I by backward steps would move,
And when this dust falls to the urn,
In that state I came, return.

Twins "Jack and Jill", early Crude Eyed, Pale Skinned
1ˢᵗ production Götz dolls from 1968
Photo by Cathy Himmel

Silentium Amoris
(The Silence of Love)
by Oscar Wilde

As often-times the too resplendent sun
Hurries the pallid and reluctant moon
Back to her sombre cave, ere she hath won
A single ballad from the nightingale,
So doth thy Beauty make my lips to fail,
And all my sweetest singing out of tune.
And as at dawn across the level mead
On wings impetuous some wind will come,
And with its too harsh kisses break the reed
Which was its only instrument of song,
So my too stormy passions work me wrong,
And for excess of Love my Love is dumb.
But surely unto Thee mine eyes did show
Why I am silent, and my lute unstrung;
Else it were better we should part, and go,
Thou to some lips of sweeter melody,
And I to nurse the barren memory
Of unkissed kisses, and songs never sung.

Sasha Repainted by Shelly Baxter
Photograph by Shelly Baxter

A BIII Studio Doll by Sasha Morgenthaler,
Photograph by Ginger Mullins

The Child's Faith is New
by Emily Dickinson

The Child's faith is new -
Whole - like His Principle -
Wide - like the Sunrise
On fresh Eyes -
Never had a Doubt -
Laughs - at a Scruple -
Believes all sham
But Paradise -
Credits the World -
Deems His Dominion
Broadest of Sovereignties -
And Caesar - mean -
In the Comparison -
Baseless Emperor -
Ruler of Nought -
Yet swaying all -
Grown bye and bye
To hold mistaken
His pretty estimates
Of Prickly Things
He gains the skill
Sorrowful - as certain -
Men - to anticipate
Instead of Kings -

Sonnet CIV
To me, fair friend, you never can be old
By William Shakespeare

To me, fair friend, you never can be old,
For as you were when first your eye I ey'd,
Such seems your beauty still. Three winters cold,
Have from the forests shook three summers' pride,

Three beauteous springs to yellow autumn turn'd,
In process of the seasons have I seen,
Three April perfumes in three hot Junes burn'd,
Since first I saw you fresh, which yet are green.

Ah! yet doth beauty like a dial-hand,
Steal from his figure, and no pace perceiv'd;
So your sweet hue, which methinks still doth stand,
Hath motion, and mine eye may be deceiv'd:

For fear of which, hear this thou age unbred:
Ere you were born was beauty's summer dead.

"Sweater" Sasha and Cora by Trendon, England
Photograph by Michele Balli Tasabia

What is the greatest gift?
by Mary Oliver
(An excerpt from Red Bird her book of poems)

What is the greatest gift?
Could it be the world itself — the oceans, the meadowlark,
the patience of the trees in the wind?
Could it be love, with its sweet clamor of passion?
Something else — something else entirely
holds me in thrall.
That you have a life that I wonder about
more than I wonder about my own.
That you have a life — courteous, intelligent —
that I wonder about more than I wonder about my own.
That you have a soul — your own, no one else's —
that I wonder about more than I wonder about my own.
So that I find my soul clapping its hands for yours
more than my own.

1968 Tiny-eyed Sasha (re-tooted)
Photograph by Leslie Anne Hendra

A Girls's Garden
By Robert Frost

A neighbor of mine in the village
Likes to tell how one spring
When she was a girl on the farm, she did
A childlike thing.

One day she asked her father
To give her a garden plot
To plant and tend and reap herself,
And he said, "Why not?"
In casting about for a corner
He thought of an idle bit
Of walled-off ground where a shop had stood,
And he said, "Just it."
And he said, "That ought to make you
An ideal one-girl farm,
And give you a chance to put some strength
On your slim-jim arm."

It was not enough of a garden,
Her father said, to plough;
So she had to work it all by hand,
But she don't mind now.
She wheeled the dung in the wheelbarrow
Along a stretch of road;
But she always ran away and left
Her not-nice load.
And hid from anyone passing.
And then she begged the seed.
She says she thinks she planted one
Of all things but weed.

A hill each of potatoes,
Radishes, lettuce, peas,
Tomatoes, beets, beans, pumpkins, corn,
And even fruit trees
And yes, she has long mistrusted
That a cider apple tree
In bearing there to-day is hers,
Or at least may be.
Her crop was a miscellany
When all was said and done,
A little bit of everything,
A great deal of none.

Now when she sees in the village
How village things go,
Just when it seems to come in right,
She says, "I know!
It's as when I was a farmer—"
Oh, never by way of advice!
And she never sins by telling the tale
To the same person twice.

Photograph by Theresa O'Neill

123

Perfect Woman
By William Wordsworth

She was a phantom of delight
When first she gleam'd upon my sight;
A lovely apparition, sent
To be a moment's ornament;
Her eyes as stars of twilight fair;
Like twilight's, too, her dusky hair;
But all things else about her drawn
From Maytime and the cheerful dawn;
A dancing shape, an image gay,
To haunt, to startle, and waylay.

I saw her upon nearer view,
A Spirit, yet a Woman too!
Her household motions light and free,
And steps of virgin liberty;
A countenance in which did meet
Sweet records, promises as sweet;
A creature not too bright or good
For human nature's daily food;
For transient sorrows, simple wiles,
Praise, blame, love, kisses, tears, and smiles.

And now I see with eye serene
The very pulse of the machine;
A being breathing thoughtful breath,
A traveller between life and death;
The reason firm, the temperate will,
Endurance, foresight, strength, and skill;

A perfect Woman, nobly plann'd,
To warm, to comfort, and command;
And yet a Spirit still, and bright
With something of angelic light.

Carrie, a Sasha restoration by Jackie Rydstrom
Photograph of by Jackie Rydstrom

La Belle Dame Sans Merci
by John Keats

O what can ail thee, knight-at-arms,
Alone and palely loitering?
The sedge has withered from the lake,
And no birds sing.
O what can ail thee, knight-at-arms,
So haggard and so woe-begone?
The squirrel's granary is full,
And the harvest's done.
I see a lily on thy brow,
With anguish moist and fever-dew,
And on thy cheeks a fading rose
Fast withereth too.
I met a lady in the meads,
Full beautiful—a faery's child,
Her hair was long, her foot was light,
And her eyes were wild.
I made a garland for her head,
And bracelets too, and fragrant zone;
She looked at me as she did love,
And made sweet moan
I set her on my pacing steed,
And nothing else saw all day long,
For sidelong would she bend, and sing
A faery's song.
She found me roots of relish sweet,
And honey wild, and manna-dew,
And sure in language strange she said—
'I love thee true'.
She took me to her Elfin grot,
And there she wept and sighed full sore,

And there I shut her wild wild eyes
With kisses four.
And there she lullèd me asleep,
And there I dreamed—Ah! woe betide!—
The latest dream I ever dreamt
On the cold hill side.
I saw pale kings and princes too,
Pale warriors, death-pale were they all;
They cried—'La Belle Dame sans Merci
Thee hath in thrall!'
I saw their starved lips in the gloam,
With horrid warning gapèd wide,
And I awoke and found me here,
On the cold hill's side.
And this is why I sojourn here,
Alone and palely loitering,
Though the sedge is withered from the lake,
And no birds sing.

Photograph by Tatyana Petrova

On Being a Woman
by Dorothy Parker

Why is it, when I am in Rome,
I'd give an eye to be at home,
But when on native earth I be,
My soul is sick for Italy?

And why with you, my love, my lord,
Am I spectacularly bored,
Yet do you up and leave me- then
I scream to have you back again?

Photograph by Theresa O'Neill

Phenomenal Woman
By Maya Angelou

Pretty women wonder where my secret lies.
I'm not cute or built to suit a fashion model's size
But when I start to tell them,
They think I'm telling lies.
I say, it's in the reach of my arms,
The span of my hips, the stride of my step,
The curl of my lips.
I'm a woman
Phenomenally.
Phenomenal woman,
That's me.

I walk into a room
Just as cool as you please,
And to a man, the fellows stand or fall down on their knees.
Then they swarm around me, a hive of honey bees.
I say, it's the fire in my eyes, and the flash of my teeth,
The swing in my waist, and the joy in my feet.
I'm a woman
Phenomenally.
Phenomenal woman,
That's me.

Men themselves have wondered what they see in me.
They try so much but they can't touch my inner mystery.
When I try to show them, they say they still can't see.
I say, it's in the arch of my back, the sun of my smile,
The ride of my breasts, the grace of my style.
I'm a woman
Phenomenally.
Phenomenal woman,

That's me.

Now you understand
Just why my head's not bowed. I don't shout or jump about
Or have to talk real loud.
When you see me passing, it ought to make you proud.
I say, it's in the click of my heels, the bend of my hair,
The palm of my hand, the need for my care.
'Cause I'm a woman
Phenomenally.
Phenomenal woman,
That's me.

Sasha Repainted and Re Wigged by Shelly Baxter
Photograph by Shelly Baxter

Mushrooms
by Sylvia Plath

Overnight, very
Whitely, discreetly,
Very quietly

Our toes, our noses
Take hold on the loam,
Acquire the air.

Nobody sees us,
Stops us, betrays us;
The small grains make room.

Soft fists insist on
Heaving the needles,
The leafy bedding,

Even the paving.
Our hammers, our rams,
Earless and eyeless,
Perfectly voiceless,
Widen the crannies,
Shoulder through holes.

We diet on water,
On crumbs of shadow,
Bland-mannered, asking
Little or nothing.
So many of us!
So many of us!

We are shelves, we are
Tables, we are meek,
We are edible,

Nudgers and shovers
In spite of ourselves.
Our kind multiplies:

We shall by morning
Inherit the earth.
Our foot's in the door.

2nd Production Götz Toddler
Photograph by Tyler Brunson O'Grady

I Wandered Lonely as a Cloud
By William Wordsworth

I wandered lonely as a cloud
That floats on high o'er vales and hills,
When all at once I saw a crowd,
A host, of golden daffodils;
Beside the lake, beneath the trees,
Fluttering and dancing in the breeze.

Continuous as the stars that shine
And twinkle on the milky way,
They stretched in never-ending line
Along the margin of a bay:
Ten thousand saw I at a glance,
Tossing their heads in sprightly dance.

The waves beside them danced; but they
Out-did the sparkling waves in glee:
A poet could not but be gay,
In such a jocund company:
I gazed—and gazed—but little thought
What wealth the show to me had brought:

For oft, when on my couch I lie
In vacant or in pensive mood,
They flash upon that inward eye
Which is the bliss of solitude;
And then my heart with pleasure fills,
And dances with the daffodils.

Photograph by Tatyana Petrova

See it Through
by Edgar Guest

When you're up against a trouble,
Meet it squarely, face to face;
Lift your chin and set your shoulders,
Plant your feet and take a brace.
When it's vain to try to dodge it,
Do the best that you can do;
You may fail, but you may conquer,
See it through!

Black may be the clouds about you
And your future may seem grim,
But don't let your nerve desert you;
Keep yourself in fighting trim.
If the worst is bound to happen,
Spite of all that you can do,
Running from it will not save you,
See it through!

Even hope may seem but futile,
When with troubles you're beset,
But remember you are facing
Just what other men have met.
You may fail, but fall still fighting;
Don't give up, whate'er you do;
Eyes front, head high to the finish.
See it through!

Sashas repainted by Shelly Baxter
Photograph by Shelly Baxter

Golden Slumbers
by Thomas Dekker

Golden slumbers kiss your eyes,
Smiles awake you when you rise;
Sleep, pretty wantons, do not cry,
And I will sing a lullaby,
Rock them, rock them, lullaby.

Care is heavy, therefore sleep you,
You are care, and care must keep you;
Sleep, pretty wantons, do not cry,
And I will sing a lullaby,
Rock them, rock them, lullaby.

2nd Production Götz
Photograph by Timnah Dockery

Sonnet 33
Full many a glorious morning have I seen
by William Shakespeare

Full many a glorious morning have I seen
Flatter the mountain tops with sovereign eye,
Kissing with golden face the meadows green,
Gilding pale streams with heavenly alchemy;
Anon permit the basest clouds to ride
With ugly rack on his celestial face,
And from the forlorn world his visage hide,
Stealing unseen to west with this disgrace:
Even so my sun one early morn did shine,
With all triumphant splendour on my brow;
But out, alack, he was but one hour mine,
The region cloud hath mask'd him from me now.
Yet him for this my love no whit disdaineth;
Suns of the world may stain when heaven's sun staineth.

1969 English Side Part Sasha
Photograph by Gillian Nash

Lullaby
by W. H. Auden

Lay your sleeping head, my love,
Human on my faithless arm;
Time and fevers burn away
Individual beauty from
Thoughtful children, and the grave
Proves the child ephemeral:
But in my arms till break of day
Let the living creature lie,
Mortal, guilty, but to me
The entirely beautiful.

Soul and body have no bounds:
To lovers as they lie upon
Her tolerant enchanted slope
In their ordinary swoon,
Grave the vision Venus sends
Of supernatural sympathy,
Universal love and hope;
While an abstract insight wakes
Among the glaciers and the rocks
The hermit's carnal ecstasy.

Certainty, fidelity
On the stroke of midnight pass
Like vibrations of a bell,
And fashionable madmen raise
Their pedantic boring cry:
Every farthing of the cost,
All the dreaded cards foretell,
Shall be paid, but from this night

Not a whisper, not a thought,
Not a kiss nor look be lost.

Beauty, midnight, vision dies:
Let the winds of dawn that blow
Softly round your dreaming head
Such a day of welcome show
Eye and knocking heart may bless,
Find the mortal world enough;
Noons of dryness find you fed
By the involuntary powers,
Nights of insult let you pass
Watched by every human love.

Photograph by Shelly Baxter

143

Winter Landscape, With Rooks
by Sylvia Plath

Water in the millrace, through a sluice of stone,
plunges headlong into that black pond
where, absurd and out-of-season, a single swan
floats chaste as snow, taunting the clouded mind
which hungers to haul the white reflection down.

The austere sun descends above the fen,
an orange cyclops-eye, scorning to look
longer on this landscape of chagrin;
feathered dark in thought, I stalk like a rook,
brooding as the winter night comes on.

Last summer's reeds are all engraved in ice
as is your image in my eye; dry frost
glazes the window of my hurt; what solace
can be struck from rock to make heart's waste
grow green again? Who'd walk in this bleak place?

1968 Single Fringe by Frido (later Trendon), England
Knitwear pattern "Llama Jacket" designed by Rosie Shortell
Photograph by Gillian Nash

Kubla Khan Or, a vision in a dream. A Fragment. By Samuel Taylor Coleridge

In Xanadu did Kubla Khan
A stately pleasure-dome decree:
Where Alph, the sacred river, ran
Through caverns measureless to man
Down to a sunless sea.
So twice five miles of fertile ground
With walls and towers were girdled round;
And there were gardens bright with sinuous rills,
Where blossomed many an incense-bearing tree;
And here were forests ancient as the hills,
Enfolding sunny spots of greenery.
But oh! that deep romantic chasm which slanted
Down the green hill athwart a cedarn cover!
A savage place! as holy and enchanted
As e'er beneath a waning moon was haunted
By woman wailing for her demon-lover!
And from this chasm, with ceaseless turmoil seething,
As if this earth in fast thick pants were breathing,
A mighty fountain momently was forced:
Amid whose swift half-intermitted burst
Huge fragments vaulted like rebounding hail,
Or chaffy grain beneath the thresher's flail:
And mid these dancing rocks at once and ever
It flung up momently the sacred river.
Five miles meandering with a mazy motion
Through wood and dale the sacred river ran,
Then reached the caverns measureless to man,
And sank in tumult to a lifeless ocean;
And 'mid this tumult Kubla heard from far
Ancestral voices prophesying war!
The shadow of the dome of pleasure
Floated midway on the waves;
Where was heard the mingled measure
From the fountain and the caves.

It was a miracle of rare device,
A sunny pleasure-dome with caves of ice!
A damsel with a dulcimer
In a vision once I saw:
It was an Abyssinian maid
And on her dulcimer she played,
Singing of Mount Abora.
Could I revive within me
Her symphony and song,
To such a deep delight 'twould win me,
That with music loud and long,
I would build that dome in air,
That sunny dome! those caves of ice!
And all who heard should see them there,
And all should cry, Beware! Beware!
His flashing eyes, his floating hair!
Weave a circle round him thrice,
And close your eyes with holy dread
For he on honey-dew hath fed,
And drunk the milk of Paradise.

Photograph and knitted wardrobe by Susanna Lewis

Holidays
By Henry Wadsworth Longfellow

The holiest of all holidays are those
Kept by ourselves in silence and apart;
The secret anniversaries of the heart,
When the full river of feeling overflows;--
The happy days unclouded to their close;
The sudden joys that out of darkness start
As flames from ashes; swift desires that dart
Like swallows singing down each wind that blows!
White as the gleam of a receding sail,
White as a cloud that floats and fades in air,
White as the whitest lily on a stream,
These tender memories are;--a fairy tale
Of some enchanted land we know not where,
But lovely as a landscape in a dream.

Outfits and bonnets made by Celia Tøsse
Photograph by Celia Tøsse

Contra Spem Spero!
(Against all hope, I hope)
by Lesya Ukrainka (**Larysa Petrivna Kosach-Kvitka**)

Away, dark thoughts, you autumn clouds!
A golden spring is here!
Shall it be thus in sorrow and in lamentation
That my youthful years pass away?

No, through all my tears I still shall laugh,
Sing songs despite my troubles;
Have hope despite all odds,
I want to live! Away, you sorrowful thoughts!

On this poor, indigent ground
I shall sow flowers of flowing colors;
I shall sow flowers even amidst the frost,
And water them with my bitter tears.

And from those burning tears will melt
The frozen crust, so hard and strong,
Perhaps the flowers will bloom and
Bring about for me a joyous spring.

Unto a winding, flinty mountain
Shall I bear my weighty stone,
Yet, even bearing such a crushing weight,
Will I sing a joyful song.

Throughout a lasting night of darkness
Ne'er shall I rest my own eyes,
Always searching for the guiding star,
The bright empress of the dark night skies.

I shall not allow my heart to fall sleep,
Though gloom and misery envelop me,
Despite my certain feelings
That death is beating at my breast.

Death will settle heavily on that breast,
The snow covered by a cruel haze,
But fierce shall beat my little heart,
And maybe, with its ferocity, overcome death.

Yes, I will laugh despite my tears,
I'll sing out songs amidst my misfortunes;
I'll have hope despite all odds,
I will live! Away, you sorrowful thoughts!

A Prayer for Ukraine
Photograph by Tyler Brunson O'Grady

151

CPSIA information can be obtained
at www.ICGtesting.com
Printed in the USA
LVHW070731270622
722151LV00019B/1